The Big Book of Mental Health for Teenagers

The Ultimate Guide to Growing, Coping & Thriving in a Digital World

Vandana Verma

DIAMOND BOOKS
www.diamondbooks.in

Publisher : **Diamond Pocket Books (P) Ltd.**
X-30, Okhla Industrial Area, Phase-II
New Delhi-110020
Phone : 011-40712200
E-mail : wecare@diamondbooks.in
Website : www.diamondbooks.in
Edition : 2025
Printed By : Repro (India)

Preface

Dear Reader,

If you're a teen who's ever felt overwhelmed, anxious, sad, left out, or simply confused by life—this book is for you.

Mental health doesn't mean you're "crazy" or "weak." It means being aware of your thoughts and feelings, and learning how to handle them in healthy ways. It's about having the confidence to ask for help and the wisdom to take care of yourself.

This book uses simple language, relatable examples, and fun tools like checklists, breathing exercises, playlists, and self-care routines. It's not a lecture—it's your personal wellness guide.

You deserve to feel mentally strong and emotionally safe. Let's begin.

With care,

- Vandana Verma

Foreword

In today's fast-changing world, being a teenager comes with enormous emotional challenges—peer pressure, academic stress, the influence of social media, identity confusion, and more. Mental health is not just a buzzword anymore—it's an urgent need, a right, and a foundation for a happy and fulfilling life.

This book was created to support teenagers like you with empathy, simplicity, and practical wisdom. Rooted in the vision of NEP 2020, it's not just a guide, but a friend in pages—walking with you through anxiety, sadness, confusion, and healing. Every chapter is crafted to speak your language and give you tools to not only cope, but to grow and thrive.

Welcome to a journey of self-awareness, strength, and emotional wellness.

INDEX

Chapter 1

What Is Mental Health?

Understanding the Basics of Your Mind and Emotions

Introduction: Why This Chapter Matters

Have you ever felt really low for no clear reason? Or maybe you've felt happy one moment and completely anxious the next? You're not alone. Our minds are powerful, and just like our bodies, they need care. Mental health isn't something "grown-ups" talk about behind closed doors—it's about you, your thoughts, your feelings, and how you deal with life.

In this chapter, we'll break down what mental health really means (in simple language), how it's different from mental illness, and why understanding it is super important—especially as a teenager in today's digital world.

5Ws of Mental Health

Let's start with the most basic and powerful tool of understanding: the 5Ws.

What is Mental Health?
Mental health refers to how you think, feel, and behave. It includes your ability to handle stress, build relationships, and make decisions. It's not just about the absence of illness, but about feeling balanced, motivated, and able to enjoy life—even when things are tough.

Think of your mind like a garden. Mental health is the sunlight, water, and soil it needs to grow. If it's dry or too crowded with weeds (negative thoughts, pressure, fear), it can affect how your flowers (happiness, focus, confidence) grow.

Why Does It Matter?

Because your brain is still growing during your teen years! This means how you think, feel, and act now can shape the kind of adult you'll become.

Good mental health:
- Helps you stay focused in school
- Improves your relationships with friends and family
- Boosts your confidence and motivation
- Keeps your body healthier too

Without it, even small problems can start to feel huge and scary.

When Should I Care About It?

Right now. Mental health isn't something you wait to fix when things go wrong—it's something you build every day. Just like brushing your teeth or eating breakfast, caring for your mind should be a habit.

You should especially care about your mental health when:

- You're feeling stressed for days or weeks
- You're having trouble sleeping, eating, or focusing
- You feel like you're not "yourself" anymore
- You just need someone to talk to

Where to Get Help?

Help is closer than you think:

- School Counselors or teachers you trust
- Parents or relatives who listen
- Mental Health Apps like Wysa or Calm
- Helplines in India like iCall, Snehi, AASRA
- Doctors, psychologists, or even peer groups

You don't have to be "sick" to seek help. Talking to someone is a strength, not a weakness.

Who Can Struggle With Mental Health?

Absolutely anyone. Mental health challenges don't care if you're rich or poor, popular or shy, good at sports or not. Even celebrities, athletes, and influencers deal with anxiety, depression, or burnout. The most important thing is to notice the signs early and take action.

Mental Health vs. Mental Illness: What's the Difference?

Let's be clear:

- Mental health is something everyone has, like physical health.
- Mental illness is when mental health problems become persistent and overwhelming, like depression, anxiety disorders, or eating disorders.

Think of it like this:

Mental Health	Mental Illness
Feeling stressed before exams	Feeling hopeless and unable to get out of bed for weeks
Getting nervous before a speech	Having frequent panic attacks
Feeling sad after a breakup	Being unable to feel joy for months

One doesn't automatically mean the other. But if left unaddressed, poor mental health can lead to illness.

Why Teens Are Especially Affected

As a teen, your brain is undergoing a major upgrade. New hormones, expectations, and responsibilities are all coming at once.

Here's what's going on:

- Your amygdala (the emotional part of the brain) becomes super active
- Your prefrontal cortex (the logical, decision-making part) is still developing
- This means emotions feel bigger, faster, and harder to control

Plus, add in:

- Academic pressure
- Relationship drama
- Body image worries
- Family expectations
- Social media comparison

...and it's easy to feel overloaded.

Real Voice

"I used to think feeling anxious or sad meant I was being 'dramatic.' But when I couldn't focus, stopped enjoying music, and felt tired all the time, I realized it was more than just mood swings. Talking to my school counselor really helped me figure things out."
— Aarav, 16, Delhi

Signs Your Mental Health Needs Attention

Check off what you relate to:

- I feel sad, anxious, or angry most of the time
- I avoid friends or activities I used to enjoy
- I'm not sleeping or eating well
- I feel worthless or unmotivated
- I find it hard to concentrate
- I've thought about harming myself

If you checked even two or more, talk to someone today. Help is real, and recovery is possible.

Try This: Quick Mind Check-In

Every evening, ask yourself:

- What emotion did I feel most today?
- What made me feel calm or happy?
- What stressed me out?
- What did I do to cope?
- What can I try tomorrow to feel better?

This is called emotional awareness—a skill that helps you understand and manage your feelings better.

Building Daily Mental Strength

Here are 5 simple daily habits that boost mental health:

Habit	Why It Works
Get sunlight	Regulates your mood and sleep cycle
Move your body	Releases happy chemicals (endorphins!)
Stay hydrated	Dehydration affects focus and energy
Journal feelings	Gets thoughts out of your head
Practice stillness	Even 5 minutes of deep breathing helps

Digital Tools That Help

Use tech to support your mind (not stress it):

App	Use
Wysa	Anonymous chatbot for emotional support
Calm	Meditation and sleep stories
ThinkRight.me	Affirmations and self-growth
Daylio	Mood tracking and journaling

Busting Mental Health Myths

× Myth	✓ Truth
"Mental illness is just drama."	No, it's a medical condition.
"Only weak people need therapy."	Strong people ask for help.
"Boys shouldn't cry."	All emotions are human. Crying is healthy.

"You can just snap out of it."	It takes time and support, not shame.

When to Get Immediate Help

If you or a friend:
• Talk about hurting themselves
• Are withdrawing from everyone
• Are acting dangerously
• Can't sleep, eat, or function

Tell a trusted adult, call a helpline, or visit a doctor. Mental health issues can't always be solved with "cheer up" quotes.

Reflection Prompt

Write down 3 things you can do this week to improve your mental wellness.

1. ______________________________
2. ______________________________
3. ______________________________

____

NEP 2020 & Mental Well-being in Schools

The National Education Policy 2020 (NEP) recognizes the importance of mental wellness alongside academics.

It promotes:
• Social-emotional learning (SEL)
• Peer mentoring
• Wellness clubs and school counselors
• Life skills training

This book is a step toward what NEP envisions—a future where teenagers are emotionally resilient and mentally empowered.

Key Takeaways

- Mental health is about how you think, feel, and act
- Everyone has mental health—even if you don't have a mental illness
- Teens go through big emotional changes due to growing brains and life pressure
- It's okay to ask for help—mental strength includes reaching out
- You can take charge of your mind through small, daily steps

Chapter 2

The Teen Brain & Growing Pains

Introduction: Why Do I Feel So Weird?

Some days you might feel like you're on top of the world—and the next, like everything is falling apart. Maybe you're angry at your parents for no clear reason or crying over something small, like a friend's late reply. Don't worry—you're not "going crazy." You're going through growing pains—emotional, physical, and mental changes that are completely normal during your teenage years. This chapter explores what's happening in your brain and body and how these changes affect your mood, confidence, energy, and even your ability to make decisions.

The Brain in Transformation

During your teenage years, your brain is like a construction site. The parts that control emotion, logic, and impulse are developing at different speeds:

Part of Brain	Function	Status in Teens
Amygdala	Handles emotions	Fully active (why emotions feel intense)
Prefrontal Cortex	Decision making & logic	Still developing till age 25
Hippocampus	Memory & learning	Active and changing
Dopamine System	Rewards & motivation	Extra sensitive (why you love risks or praise)

So when you feel super emotional or act without thinking—it's biology, not bad behavior.

Hormones, Puberty, and Mood Swings

Puberty hits like a thunderstorm—often sudden, messy, and powerful.
• Hormones like estrogen, testosterone, and cortisol start flowing through your body
• They change your physical body (height, voice, body hair, etc.)
• They also affect your mood, sleep, and emotional control

You might feel:
• Angry or irritable for no reason
• Sad or insecure
• Overexcited or restless
• Tired but unable to sleep
This rollercoaster is normal. But learning to understand and manage your emotions gives you power over the storm.

Identity: Who Am I Really?

Teenage years are all about figuring out who you are. This includes:
• What you believe in
• What career or passions you want

• Who your friends are
• How you express yourself (fashion, opinions, lifestyle)
This search can sometimes feel overwhelming—especially if you don't "fit in" or if people expect you to act a certain way.

You may ask:
• Am I cool enough?
• Do I look good enough?
• Should I change to be accepted?
These are common questions. But remember, the most powerful identity is one that is authentic—being yourself, not who others expect you to be.

Peer Pressure and FOMO

Your brain is more sensitive to social feedback during your teens.

That's why:
• A rude comment from a friend hurts deeply
• A "like" on social media feels rewarding
• Being left out gives you FOMO (Fear of Missing Out)
This doesn't mean you're weak. It means your brain is learning how to socially adapt. But too much pressure to "be like others" can make you lose your sense of self.

Try This: Write down 3 things that make you uniquely YOU. These could be your sense of humor, your curiosity, your kindness. Celebrate them.

Sleep Struggles: Why You're Always Tired

Your sleep cycle shifts during adolescence. That's why:
• You may feel sleepy at 2 a.m.
• But need to wake up early for school

This mismatch makes you feel:
- Grumpy or emotional
- Unfocused in class
- More prone to anxiety or sadness

Solution:
Aim for 8–9 hours of sleep. Create a digital curfew—no screens 1 hour before bed. Use a soft playlist, eye mask, or breathing app like Calm to help you wind down.

Food and Mood: What You Eat Affects How You Feel

Teen brains need fuel—but not just any fuel.

If you're eating:
- Chips and sugar all day
- Skipping breakfast
- Drinking too much caffeine

You might notice:
- Mood crashes
- Low energy
- Trouble concentrating

Instead, try these brain-boosting foods:

Eat This	For This Benefit
Nuts & seeds	Healthy brain function
Fruits & veggies	Stable mood & energy
Whole grains	Better focus
Water	Less fatigue & headaches

Try This: Start your day with a "Power Plate" — a mix of protein (eggs/daal), carbs (toast/roti), and fruit.

Move That Body, Lift Your Mood

Exercise isn't just for fitness—it's a secret weapon for mental health.

When you move your body:
- Your brain releases endorphins (natural happy chemicals)
- Your stress levels drop
- Your confidence increases

You don't have to join a gym. Try:
- Dancing in your room
- Playing gully cricket
- Walking around your block
- Yoga or skipping

Even 15 minutes a day makes a huge difference.

Real Voice

"When I started doing 20 minutes of yoga every morning, I didn't expect much. But within a week, I was sleeping better, smiling more, and snapping less at my siblings. It's like my brain had more space to breathe."
— Ritika, 15, Pune

Quick Mood Journal (Try for 5 Days)

Create a table in your notebook like this:

Day	Mood (1–10)	Sleep (hrs)	Exercise? (Y/N)	Biggest Emotion
Monday				
Tuesday				

At the end of the week, reflect:
What patterns do you notice?
How does sleep or food change your mood?
What helped you stay calm?

Brain-Friendly Apps

App	Why Use It
Headspace	Animated lessons on stress, sleep, focus
Youper	AI-powered journaling & emotional check-ins
MyLife	Guided meditations for teens
SleepTown	Build a virtual town by sticking to sleep goals

Balancing Emotions: The 3-Minute Rule

Next time you feel overwhelmed, try this:
1. **STOP** – Put down your phone or walk away from the situation
2. **BREATHE** – 10 deep belly breaths
3. **NAME IT** – Say what you're feeling: "I'm anxious," "I'm annoyed"
4. **MOVE** – Stretch, jump, or take a short walk
5. **WRITE** – Jot down one helpful thing you can do next

These small steps help you create emotional distance before reacting.

What to Expect from Yourself

Here's the truth: You're still becoming. You won't always have the answers. You might mess up. You'll change your mind, maybe even your goals. And that's okay.

Instead of chasing perfection, aim for:
- Progress, not perfection
- Effort, not applause
- Curiosity, not comparison

Reflection Prompt

Write a letter to your future self (age 25).

- What do you want them to remember about these years?
- What habits do you hope they've kept?
- What makes you proud of who you are today?

Key Takeaways

- Your teenage brain is still developing, especially areas that control emotion and judgment
- Hormones, identity changes, and social pressure are part of growing up—but they don't define you
- Small habits like good sleep, movement, and food can help balance mood
- You're not "too emotional"—you're human and learning
- Self-awareness is the first step to emotional strength

Chapter 3

Anxiety

The Fast Heart & Racing Mind

Introduction: When Worry Takes Over

Have you ever felt your heart beating fast before an exam? Or sweaty palms before speaking in class? Maybe you couldn't sleep because your mind was replaying a moment again and again. That's anxiety—and believe it or not, it's something everyone experiences.
But when anxiety becomes too frequent, intense, or hard to control, it starts affecting your life. This chapter breaks down what anxiety is, how to recognize it, and how to manage it like a pro, even in this fast-moving, hyperconnected world.

What Is Anxiety?

Anxiety is your body's natural alarm system. It's what helped our ancestors survive—like running from danger. But in today's world,

anxiety gets triggered by exams, social media, family fights, and even imagined fears.
So anxiety is not bad—it's your brain trying to protect you. The problem is when the alarm keeps going off even when there's no real danger.

The 5Ws of Anxiety

Let's break anxiety down into the 5Ws.

What is Anxiety?
Anxiety is a feeling of fear, nervousness, or worry about what's coming next—even if you don't know what exactly.

It shows up in:
• **Thoughts** – "What if I fail?" "What if they laugh at me?"
• **Body** – racing heart, dry mouth, sweating, shaky hands
• **Behavior** – avoiding people, biting nails, overstudying, checking things repeatedly

Why Does It Happen?
Because your brain is trying to protect you from danger or failure.

But sometimes it overreacts to situations like:
• Upcoming exams
• Being judged by others
• Trying something new
• Dealing with pressure at home or online

Anxiety comes from the amygdala part of your brain that sends out a "fight, flight, or freeze" signal.

When Should I Care?

It's normal to feel nervous sometimes. But watch out if:
• You're anxious almost every day

• Worry stops you from sleeping, eating, or going out
• You avoid people, places, or events
• You feel like you're always on edge
This means anxiety is starting to control you, and it's time to take action.

Where Can I Feel It?

Anxiety can affect your whole body:

Area	Effect
Chest	Tightness, rapid heartbeat
Head	Headaches, overthinking
Stomach	Nausea, "butterflies"
Muscles	Tension, restlessness
Hands	Sweating, shaking

Who Gets Anxious?
Everyone. Even the most confident people.
Athletes feel anxious before a match. Artists get nervous before performing. Students worry before tests. Influencers panic over social media pressure.

You are not alone in this.

Types of Anxiety Teens Experience

Let's name it to tame it:

1. General Anxiety:
Constant worrying about many things—school, friends, health.
2. **Social Anxiety:**
Fear of being judged, laughed at, or embarrassed in front of others.
3. **Performance Anxiety:**

Stress over doing well in exams, sports, or public speaking.
4. **Test Anxiety:**
Freezing, blanking out, or feeling sick during tests—even after preparing.
5. **Health Anxiety:**
Obsessing over minor symptoms, fearing illness.

Anxiety Symptom Checklist

Mark the ones you relate to:

- Racing heartbeat
- Feeling breathless or dizzy
- Constant worry or overthinking
- Trouble sleeping
- Avoiding people or events
- Stomach pain, nausea
- Feeling restless or easily tired
- Mind going blank
- Feeling like something bad will happen

If you checked 3 or more, it's time to build your anxiety toolbox.

Try This: Box Breathing

Box breathing is a simple technique that calms your brain in 1 minute.

Step-by-step:

- Inhale for 4 counts
- Hold for 4 counts
- Exhale for 4 counts
- Hold again for 4 counts

Repeat this 4 times. Close your eyes and imagine drawing a square with your breath. This slows your heart rate and brings back focus.

Try This: Grounding 5-4-3-2-1

Feeling like your mind is racing? Use your senses to come back to the present:

- 5 things you can see
- 4 things you can touch
- 3 things you can hear
- 2 things you can smell
- 1 thing you can taste

This technique is great for panic, overthinking, and social anxiety.

Real Voice

"Before exams, I used to feel like I couldn't breathe. My chest would tighten, and I felt like crying. Then I learned grounding techniques. I now carry a small pebble in my pocket—when I touch it, I remember to breathe. It's my anchor."
— **Kunal, 17, Lucknow**

Apps That Help

App	Feature
Wysa	Chat with an AI coach about your feelings
Calm	Anxiety meditations, relaxing music
MindShift	Teen-friendly tips for anxiety and panic
Breathe2Relax	Step-by-step guided breathing

Affirmations to Calm the Mind

Speak or write these to yourself:

- "This feeling will pass."
- "I am safe in this moment."
- "I can handle this one step at a time."

• "Anxiety is a signal, not a sentence."
• "I am doing my best, and that is enough."

Repeat 2–3 affirmations every morning or whenever you feel tense.

Quick Daily Habits to Reduce Anxiety

Habit	Why It Works
Stretch or move	Releases tension from your body
Journal your thoughts	Helps release worry from your head
Get sunlight	Improves mood and energy
Listen to calm music	Soothes the nervous system
Drink water	Dehydration increases anxiety symptoms

Do's and Don'ts for Anxiety

✓Do This	×Avoid This
Talk to someone you trust	Keeping it all inside
Focus on your breath	Constantly checking your phone
Use calming tools	Caffeine or energy drinks
Challenge anxious thoughts	Believing every fear is true
Take breaks	Overloading yourself

"What If" vs. "What Is"

Most anxiety is future-based:
• "What if I fail?"
• "What if they laugh at me?"

Instead, practice present-based thinking:
• "What is happening right now?"
• "Am I safe in this moment?"

• "What can I control?"

Shifting to the now helps reduce the what ifs.

NEP 2020 and Emotional Resilience

The NEP 2020 encourages schools to:

• Integrate life skills like emotional awareness and coping skills
• Provide counselors and peer support clubs
• Make well-being part of everyday learning

This book, and this chapter, are your tools to become more aware, prepared, and in control of your emotions.

Reflection Prompt

Write about a time when you felt really anxious.

• What triggered it?
• What helped you feel better?
• What can you do next time to manage it early?

Key Takeaways

• Anxiety is normal, but too much of it can disrupt your life
• It shows up in thoughts, body, and behavior
• Box breathing, grounding, and journaling are simple ways to cope
• You're not alone—everyone feels anxious sometimes
• Help is available through people, apps, and healthy habits

Chapter 4

Depression

More Than Just Sadness

Introduction: Is It Just a Bad Day?

It's normal to feel down sometimes—maybe after a fight with a friend, a poor grade, or just a rough week. But what happens when that sadness doesn't go away? When you don't want to get out of bed, don't enjoy things you used to love, and feel like there's no point in trying anymore? That's not just being moody. It might be depression.

This chapter helps you understand what depression is (and isn't), how it feels, and what to do when the sadness feels too heavy to carry.

What Is Depression?

Depression is a serious mental health condition that affects how you think, feel, and act. It's not the same as feeling sad. Sadness comes and goes. Depression lingers and makes it hard to enjoy life—even the good parts.

5Ws of Depression

Let's break down depression through the 5Ws to better understand it.

What is Depression?
Depression is a state of persistent low mood, loss of interest, and lack of motivation, often lasting for weeks or longer.

It can affect:
• Your emotions (feeling hopeless, empty, irritated)
• Your body (fatigue, sleep issues, appetite changes)
• Your thoughts (negative thinking, low self-worth)
• Your behavior (isolation, quitting hobbies)

It's not "just being lazy" or "dramatic." It's real. It's serious. And it's treatable.

Why Does It Happen?

There's no single reason—but common triggers include:
• Major life changes (divorce, moving, breakups)
• Academic pressure or failure
• Constant criticism or bullying
• Loss of a loved one
• Loneliness or lack of support
• Chronic stress or anxiety

Biology matters too—chemical imbalances in the brain and family history can play a role.

When Should I Care?

When sadness lasts more than 2 weeks and interferes with your:
• Schoolwork
• Friendships

• Sleep or eating habits
• Motivation to do basic things
That's when it's time to take it seriously.

Where Can It Affect You?

Depression can affect every part of life—school, family, hobbies, friendships, self-image. You may:
• Stop talking to friends
• Quit your favorite sport
• Feel numb even at celebrations
• Lose interest in personal hygiene
It doesn't always look like crying. Sometimes it's just feeling nothing.

Who Can Experience It?
Anyone—yes, even teens who seem "happy" or "successful."

Some warning signs might be subtle:
• Smiling less
• Being unusually quiet
• Always tired
• Saying things like "I'm tired of everything" or "It doesn't matter anymore"
Depression doesn't discriminate.

Depression Symptom Checklist

Mark any of these that apply for more than 2 weeks:
• I feel sad or empty most of the day
• I've lost interest in things I used to enjoy
• I'm always tired or sleepy
• I eat too much or too little
• I feel hopeless or worthless
• I find it hard to concentrate
• I avoid people

- I've thought about death or hurting myself

Checking 3 or more? You may be experiencing clinical depression—and it's time to seek help.

Real Voice

"At first, I thought I was just stressed. Then I realized I hadn't laughed in weeks. I was always exhausted and didn't care about school or friends anymore. Talking to a counselor helped me realize I wasn't alone—and that I could feel better."
— Simran, 16, Mumbai

Myths vs. Facts

×Myth	✓ Fact
"Depression is just sadness."	It's a medical condition that affects your whole life.
"Only adults get depressed."	1 in 4 teens show signs of depression.
"It's all in your head."	It affects your body, sleep, appetite, and energy too.
"People with depression are weak."	Asking for help takes incredible courage.

Try This: Mood Tracker Activity

Track your mood every day for one week.

Day	Mood (1–10)	Energy Level	Sleep Hours	Notes
Mon				
Tue				

After 7 days, reflect:
• What patterns do you see?
• Which days felt better, and why?
• What helped your mood improve?

Small Habits, Big Help

You don't need to do everything at once. Just pick one thing a day:

Action	Effect
Open the curtains	Let in natural light, boosts mood
Walk for 15 minutes	Movement boosts serotonin
Talk to one person	Reduces isolation
Take a shower	Refreshes body and mind

Eat something nourishing Fuels your brain and body
Even tiny wins count.

Apps for Depression Support

App	Purpose
Daylio	Track your mood and activities
Wysa	Anonymous chatbot for support
Happify	Build happiness with science-based games
Calm Harm	Manage self-harm urges safely

How to Ask for Help (With Script!)

Talking about depression can feel scary. Here's a simple script:
"I haven't been feeling like myself lately. I feel low most of the time, and I think I need someone to talk to. Can you help me find support?"

Say it to a parent, teacher, counselor, or adult you trust.

If you can't say it out loud, write it in a note or message. Asking for help is step one toward healing.

Try This: 5-Minute Reset

1. Sit comfortably and close your eyes
2. Inhale deeply for 4 seconds
3. Hold for 4 seconds
4. Exhale slowly for 6 seconds
5. Do this for 2–3 rounds
6. **Now, place your hand on your heart and say:**
    - "This is tough, but I'm tougher."
    - "I deserve peace. I am enough."

Positive Affirmations for Dark Days

- "My feelings are valid."
- "I am not my depression."
- "Healing takes time, and that's okay."
- "I am not alone."
- "There is hope, even if I don't feel it now."

What To Say to a Friend Who's Depressed

- "I'm here if you want to talk."
- "You're not alone."
- "It's okay not to be okay."
- "Would you like me to go with you to talk to someone?"

Avoid:
- "Just cheer up."
- "Others have it worse."
- "You're being too sensitive."

When Depression Gets Dangerous

If someone:

- Talks about wanting to die
- Mentions self-harm
- Gives away their belongings
- Says things like "The world would be better without me"

Take it seriously.

- Don't leave them alone
- Tell a trusted adult immediately
- Call a helpline: iCall (9152987821), AASRA (91-22-27546669)

Saving a life is more important than keeping a secret.

NEP 2020 and Depression Support in Schools

The NEP 2020 encourages:

- Emotional well-being programs in schools
- Access to trained counselors
- Wellness clubs for peer connection
- De-stigmatizing mental health conversations

Your mental health is as important as your marks.

Reflection Prompt

Write a message to your future self. What do you want them to remember if they ever feel this way again?

- "You got through it once, you can do it again."
- "You are loved, even when you can't feel it."
- "This darkness is temporary—light is coming."

Key Takeaways

• Depression is more than sadness—it affects your thoughts, energy, and behavior
• Anyone can experience it, even teens
• Tracking your mood, small habits, and support systems help
• Asking for help is a brave and essential first step
• You're not alone, and there is always hope and healing ahead

Chapter 5

Panic Attacks

Out of Nowhere

Introduction: When Fear Hits Like a Storm

Have you ever felt like your heart is pounding, your chest is tight, your hands are shaking, and you can't breathe—but nothing is really happening around you?

That may have been a panic attack. And you're not alone.

Panic attacks can feel terrifying. But they are not dangerous, and with the right tools, you can learn to manage them, reduce their frequency, and feel more in control.

This chapter breaks it all down—what panic attacks are, why they happen, and exactly what to do when one strikes.

5Ws of Panic Attacks

Let's begin by understanding panic attacks through the 5Ws framework.

What Is a Panic Attack?
A panic attack is a sudden wave of overwhelming fear or anxiety, often for no clear reason. It usually peaks within 10–15 minutes but can leave you shaken afterward.
During a panic attack, your body behaves like it's facing a life-or-death emergency—even when you're just sitting in class or lying in bed.

Common symptoms include:
- Racing heart
- Trouble breathing
- Sweating or chills
- Feeling dizzy or faint
- Chest pain or tightness
- Tingling or numbness
- Fear of losing control or "going crazy"

Why Does It Happen?
Panic attacks are triggered by your brain's fight-or-flight response. Something (a thought, memory, or even nothing noticeable) tells your brain, "You're in danger!"
Your brain releases adrenaline, your heart speeds up, and your body gets ready to fight or run—even though no real danger is present.

Common triggers:
- Intense stress
- Past trauma
- Social pressure
- Overthinking
- Caffeine or poor sleep

Sometimes, there's no clear reason at all—and that's what makes panic attacks so confusing.

When Should I Care?
A panic attack once in a while might just be a stress response.

But if you:
• Have frequent attacks
• Avoid places in fear of having one
• Feel scared of "losing control" often
• Feel like your life is being limited by fear

You might have Panic Disorder, and it's time to talk to a counselor or doctor.

Where Can They Happen?
Anywhere. That's what makes them scary.
• In the middle of class
• At home, in bed
• While eating or studying
• Even in safe, happy environments

It's the brain sending wrong signals, not the place itself that's dangerous.

Who Can Get Them?
Anyone.
• Teens going through tough academic or family situations
• Kids recovering from trauma or bullying
• Highly sensitive, overthinking personalities
• Even confident, outgoing teens can experience panic

It's not about weakness—it's about how your brain reacts to stress.

Real Voice

"The first time I had a panic attack, I thought I was dying. My chest hurt, and I couldn't catch my breath. The more I panicked, the worse it got. My teacher helped me breathe through it, and later I learned it was a panic attack—not a heart attack."
— Mehul, 17, Chandigarh

How to Recognize a Panic Attack

Physical Signs	Mental Signs
Rapid heartbeat	Fear of dying or fainting
Shortness of breath	Feeling of losing control
Trembling or shaking	"I need to escape right now"
Sweating/chills	Feeling detached from surroundings (derealization)
Dizziness/nausea	Racing thoughts or mental fog

What to Do During a Panic Attack

When panic hits, here's a simple toolbox of calming techniques:
5-4-3-2-1 Grounding

This uses your senses to bring your focus to the present.
• 5 things you can see
• 4 things you can touch
• 3 things you can hear
• 2 things you can smell
• 1 thing you can taste

It helps your brain feel safe by reactivating the logical part of your mind.

Box Breathing

Breathe in a square shape:
• **Inhale:** 4 seconds
• **Hold:** 4 seconds
• **Exhale:** 4 seconds
• **Hold:** 4 seconds
Repeat for 4 rounds while imagining drawing a square with your

breath. This slows your heart rate and calms your nerves.

The Butterfly Hug

- Cross your arms over your chest like an "X"
- Place your hands on your shoulders
- Gently tap one side, then the other
- Breathe in rhythm while tapping for 1–2 minutes

This technique is calming and especially helpful for anxiety linked to past trauma or overwhelm.

Tech Tools That Help

App	Function
MindShift	Panic survival tools, thought-challenging exercises
Breathe+	Visual breathing guides
Wysa	AI-powered support and calming activities
Calm Harm	Strategies to manage overwhelming emotions safely

Panic Attack Action Plan

Create a "Just in Case" note for yourself. Here's an example you can customize:

Dear Me,

If you're having a panic attack right now:

- **Remember:** This is temporary.
- You are safe. You are not in danger.
- **Breathe slowly:** In 4, hold 4, out 4.
- **Look around:** What can you see and touch?
- Text someone if you need support.
- This will pass. You've survived it before.

Stick it in your notebook, wallet, or phone.

Do's and Don'ts When Helping a Friend

Do This	Don't Do This
Stay calm and speak gently	Say "Relax!" or "Calm down!" forcefully
Guide them through breathing	Ask them too many questions
Let them know they're safe	Crowd them or attract attention
Offer water or space	Make them feel embarrassed or ashamed
Stay with them until it passes	Leave them alone in panic

Music, Scents & Touch: Hidden Calming Tools

Sometimes panic can be eased by sensory regulation:

• **Music:** Create a calm playlist with slow, familiar songs

• **Scents:** Lavender, sandalwood, or lemon can be soothing

• **Touch:** Holding a soft object, cold water on hands, or stress balls can distract the brain from panic

Try This: Keep a "Calm Kit" in your school bag:

• Small stress ball

• Earbuds + calming playlist

• A comforting photo

• Lavender roll-on

• Positive affirmations card

Reflection Prompt

Think back to a time you felt very anxious or panicked.

• What helped you calm down?

• What didn't help?

• What would you like someone to say to you next time?
Writing helps process fear in a safe, quiet space.

NEP 2020 and Panic Education

The NEP 2020 emphasizes:

• Safe emotional environments in schools
• Trained wellness coordinators and counselors
• Peer-led wellness clubs
• Integration of stress management and breathing practices in the school day

Understanding panic is not just about calming down—it's about creating systems of support.

Try This: Create Your Own "Safe Circle"

Draw a circle and list 5 people you can reach out to when panic strikes:

• 1 trusted adult
• 1 friend
• 1 school counselor or teacher
• 1 helpline or support service
• 1 safe space (library, music room, terrace)

This becomes your support map.

Key Takeaways

• Panic attacks are sudden, intense episodes of fear that feel real but are not harmful
• Your brain and body are reacting to perceived danger
• Grounding, breathing, and sensory tools help calm you down
• You're not alone—millions of teens experience panic
• With awareness and support, you can manage panic and reclaim your calm

Chapter 6

Tech & Mental Health

Friend or Foe?

Introduction: Always Online, But Still Stressed?

Let's be honest—technology is everywhere. From the moment you wake up to when you go to bed, you're probably scrolling, texting, watching, gaming, or creating. And while all of this can be fun, it can also make you feel tired, distracted, anxious, or even sad.
So the question is—is tech helping or hurting your mental health? In this chapter, we'll explore the good, the bad, and how to find balance in a digital world that never hits pause.

5Ws of Tech & Mental Health

Let's break it down using the 5Ws framework.

What is the Connection Between Tech & Mental Health?
Technology itself isn't good or bad—it's a tool. How we use it

determines how it affects our mental health.
• Healthy use = connection, learning, expression
• Unhealthy use = anxiety, comparison, poor sleep, social withdrawal

Think of tech like food—too much junk, and it affects your energy. The same goes for digital junk.

Why Does It Matter?

Because teens today are spending 6 to 9 hours daily on screens. While some of that is educational or creative, a large chunk is:
• Scrolling through social media
• Watching short videos on loop
• Playing competitive online games
• Comparing your life with others online

This nonstop digital diet impacts your:
• Attention span
• Sleep quality
• Self-esteem
• Stress levels

When Does Tech Start to Hurt?

Red flags include:
• You feel anxious when you're not online
• You check your phone even when nothing's happening
• You sleep less because of screen time
• You feel bad about your body or life after scrolling
• You start ignoring offline friendships

If you said "yes" to even 3 of these, it's time to rethink your digital habits.

Where Does the Impact Show Up?

Area of Life	Effect of Overuse
Sleep	Less REM sleep, brain fatigue
Mood	Anxiety, sadness, irritability
Body	Eye strain, poor posture, headaches
Focus	Shorter attention span, distraction in class
Self-worth	Comparison with edited, filtered lives

Who Is Affected?

Every teen—yes, even you.

• Gamers feel pressure to perform
• Social media users feel FOMO and comparison
• Study apps can become distractions
• Even "digital detoxers" feel left out at times

You're not alone if you've struggled with tech overload.

Real Voice

"I used to wake up and check Instagram within 2 minutes. I didn't even brush my teeth first. I felt like my self-worth depended on likes and DMs. Eventually, I noticed I was always tired, anxious, and comparing myself to people I didn't even know. Now, I take 30-minute screen breaks and leave my phone in another room at night. It really helps."
— Mahi, 16, Bengaluru

The Dark Side: Social Media & Mental Health

While social media helps you connect,

It also causes:

Comparison Culture

• Seeing influencers with "perfect" lives, bodies, relationships
• Feeling like you're not good enough or missing out

FOMO (Fear of Missing Out)

- “Everyone else is having fun—except me.”
- You start going to places or doing things just to post them

Cyberbullying

- Mean comments, exclusion, rumors, or private info being shared
- Even silence (being “left on seen”) can hurt emotionally

Pressure to Perform

- Looking perfect on every selfie
- Making sure every story or reel is cool, trendy, or funny
- Anxiety when posts don’t get likes or views

The Bright Side: Tech That Heals

Tech can also be your friend!

- Apps that teach you to meditate, reflect, and journal
- Platforms that let you create art, music, writing
- Videos that inspire you to grow, heal, or laugh
- Games that help you solve problems or build teamwork
- Online communities where you find support, not shame

It’s all about how you use it.

Try This: Create a Digital Wellness Plan

Design your own Digital Wellness Planner using these steps:

1. Track Your Time

Use apps like Digital Wellbeing (Android) or Screen Time (iOS) to check how much time you spend where.

- **Social Media:** ____________ hrs/day
- **Gaming:** ________________ hrs/day
- **Messaging:** ______________ hrs/day
- **Learning/Productive:** _________ hrs/day

2. Identify Energy Drainers

Ask: What apps leave me feeling tired, anxious, or low?
Highlight 2–3 apps to limit or set boundaries for.

3. Set Boundaries

Try:
- No screens 1 hour before bed
- Social media only between 5–6 PM
- Turn off notifications for non-urgent apps
- "Do Not Disturb" during study time

4. Replace With Real-Life Joy
- Read for 10 minutes
- Go for a walk
- Dance to your favorite music
- Do nothing—just rest!

Try This: The "Scroll Break" Challenge

Every time you feel like scrolling mindlessly:
1. Stop.
2. Take 3 deep breaths.
3. **Ask:** Why do I want to scroll right now?
    - o Am I bored?
    - o Avoiding something?
    - o Looking for validation?

Then decide: Can I do something else instead?

Even replacing 1 scroll session per day with a healthy habit makes a big difference.

Wellness Apps Worth Downloading

App	Why It's Helpful
Wysa	Anonymous AI chatbot for anxiety, stress, low mood
Forest	Stay focused by growing a digital tree when off-screen
Fabulous	Build healthy morning & evening routines
Youper	Emotional health assistant that tracks feelings & patterns
ThinkRight.me	Indian app with guided affirmations and focus tools

"Tech Check" Self-Reflection

Answer these honestly:

- Do I use my phone as a way to avoid difficult emotions?
- Am I comparing my life with others' highlight reels?
- Do I check my phone before brushing my teeth in the morning?
- Have I felt sad, angry, or jealous because of something I saw online?
- Can I spend 30 minutes alone without checking a screen?

If you answered "yes" to 3 or more, it's time to hit pause and reflect.

Digital Detox: How to Start

A digital detox doesn't mean quitting everything. It means taking back control.

Try:

- 24 hours without social media
- No phones during meals or family time
- Tech-free zone: your study table or bedroom
- "Slow Sundays" with no screen scrolling till 12 noon

Start small. The goal is freedom, not punishment.

Reflection Prompt

Journal:

- How does my phone use affect my mood?
- What's one app I'd like to use more mindfully?
- What could I do with 1 extra hour if I wasn't on my phone?

NEP 2020 and Digital Wellness

The National Education Policy 2020 includes:

- Digital literacy education
- Promoting balance between screen time and physical activity
- Encouraging use of ed-tech for learning, not overuse
- Training students on digital citizenship and responsibility

Your mental health in the digital world matters—and the system is adapting to support that.

Key Takeaways

- Tech is a powerful tool—it can both help and hurt your mental health
- Overuse leads to anxiety, FOMO, sleep issues, and self-esteem problems
- Creating screen-time boundaries and using healing apps helps restore balance
- Small steps like scroll breaks, detox days, and replacing digital time with real-life activities can reduce stress
- You are in control of your screen—not the other way around

Chapter 7

Coping With Change & Pressure

Introduction: Life Keeps Changing—And That's Okay

One minute you're laughing with your friends, and the next, you're feeling overwhelmed by homework, confused about your future, or upset about a sudden change. Whether it's exams, shifting friendships, breakups, failure, or unexpected news—change is part of life.
But here's the thing: even if we can't stop change, we can learn how to cope with it, manage the pressure, and grow stronger from it.
In this chapter, we'll explore the mental health impact of stress, how to recognize when pressure gets too much, and what real tools you can use to handle it all—without falling apart.

5Ws of Stress and Change

Let's understand the emotional rollercoaster of change using the 5Ws.
What is Stress?
Stress is your body's response to pressure—when you feel like you have too much to do, too many emotions, or too little control.

A little stress = motivation (like before a test)
Too much stress = burnout, anxiety, and breakdowns

Change adds stress because it often comes with uncertainty—and your brain doesn't like not knowing what's next.

Why Do We Feel Stressed During Change?
Because your brain is wired to protect you from danger—even emotional danger.
When something unfamiliar happens (like losing a friend or getting low marks), your brain goes into "alert mode."

You might:
- Overthink
- Get moody
- Avoid people
- Feel drained
- Experience body pain or fatigue

It's your brain saying: "I don't feel safe." But with the right tools, you can show your brain that it's okay to adjust.

When Does Pressure Become a Problem?
When it goes from "I need to try hard" to "I'm not good enough."

When it starts affecting your:
- Sleep
- Appetite
- Motivation
- Relationships
- Health

Some signs:
- You can't relax, even during free time
- You constantly feel behind

- You beat yourself up over small mistakes
- You cry often or feel numb

Where Does Stress Show Up in Teens?

Trigger	Impact
Board exams	Insomnia, fear, overstudying, guilt
Changing schools	Loneliness, insecurity
Breakups	Sadness, low confidence, obsession
Losing a friend	Anger, confusion, grief
Academic failure	Shame, self-doubt, hopelessness
Parents' pressure	Anxiety, rebellion, withdrawal

Who Can Help You Cope?

You don't have to do it all alone. Try:

- Talking to a trusted adult
- Reaching out to a school counselor
- Journaling your thoughts
- Talking to a friend who listens without judgment
- Joining a support group or teen wellness club

Even one empathetic conversation can make a huge difference.

Real Voice

"When I failed a subject in Class 11, I felt like a total loser. My parents were disappointed, and I just wanted to disappear. But a teacher told me, 'This is just a moment, not your whole story.' That sentence changed everything. I studied smart, not hard, and passed with confidence the next year."

— Nikhil, 17, Jaipur

What Does Stress Do to the Body?

Body Part	Effect of Stress
Brain	Foggy thinking, overthinking, headaches
Heart	Faster heartbeat, chest tightness
Muscles	Tension in shoulders, neck, jaw
Stomach	Nausea, indigestion, lack of appetite
Skin	Acne, rashes, dryness

Positive Coping vs. Negative Coping

Positive Coping	Negative Coping
Talking it out	Bottling it up
Exercising or stretching	Staying in bed all day
Journaling or creative expression	Hurting yourself
Deep breathing and meditation	Yelling at others
Reframing failure as feedback	Calling yourself "useless"

Your brain learns from how you cope. Choose wisely.

Try This: Gratitude Jar

When everything feels like it's going wrong, try this daily habit:

1. Get a small jar and paper slips
2. Every evening, write one good thing from the day
3. **It could be:** "Friend smiled at me," "Ate my favorite food," "Sunset looked pretty"
4. Drop it into the jar
5. Open the jar on a bad day—you'll remember things do get better

Vision Board for Life Goals

When life feels messy, having a vision gives you hope.

Make a vision board:
- Cut out or draw pictures of your goals
- Add quotes that inspire you
- Add your name in big, bold letters
- Place it where you can see it daily

This helps your brain stay focused on what matters, not just what's happening right now.

When You "Fail": Rethinking the F-Word

Failure doesn't mean the end—it means something didn't go as planned.

Instead of thinking:
- ✗ "I failed, I'm a loser"

Think:
- ✓ "I failed, so now I know what not to do next time."

Examples of famous failures:
- APJ Abdul Kalam failed to become a pilot—he became the Missile Man of India instead
- J.K. Rowling was rejected by 12 publishers before Harry Potter got published

It's not about never failing—it's about never quitting.

Breathing Exercise: The "Flower and Candle"

When you feel overwhelmed:
- Imagine a flower in one hand, a candle in the other
- Breathe in like you're smelling the flower

- Breathe out like you're blowing out the candle
- Repeat for 2 minutes

This resets your nervous system.

Helpful Apps

App	Why Use It
Fabulous	Build healthy routines step-by-step
Headspace	Simple meditation for stress and focus
Journify	Voice journal your thoughts on the go
Daylio	Track your mood and daily achievements
Woebot	AI chatbot to coach you through emotions

What to Say to a Stressed Friend

- "You're not alone. Want to talk?"
- "Let's figure this out together."
- "I see how hard you're trying."
- "This moment doesn't define you."

Avoid saying:

- "It's not a big deal."
- "Why are you overreacting?"
- "You should have tried harder."

Support can be silent, too—just being there counts.

NEP 2020 & Managing Life Skills

The National Education Policy (NEP) 2020 supports:

- Life skills and emotional well-being in school curriculum
- Training teachers to recognize stress in students
- Promoting resilience, not just test performance

• Encouraging co-curricular activities for stress release
You're allowed to take care of your mind while building your future.

Reflection Prompt

Write down:
• One thing that's stressing me right now is: _______
• One small action I can take today: _______
• Someone I can talk to about it: _______

Sometimes writing helps more than overthinking.

Key Takeaways

• Change and pressure are part of life, but you can learn to handle them
• Not all stress is bad—but too much can harm your mental health
• Coping skills like journaling, vision boards, movement, and breathing help
• You're not defined by failure—you're defined by your comeback
• You have the power to respond, reflect, and rise stronger

Chapter 8

Body Image & Self-Worth

Introduction: Do You Like What You See in the Mirror?

Have you ever looked in the mirror and wished you looked different? Maybe you've compared yourself to someone on social media or felt pressure to fit into a certain size, shape, or style. If you've felt this way—you're not alone.

Teenagers everywhere struggle with body image and self-worth, especially in today's world of filters, followers, and flawless selfies. This chapter will help you understand where these feelings come from, how to challenge them, and how to start seeing yourself through a kinder lens.

5Ws of Body Image & Self-Worth

Let's explore body image and confidence through the 5Ws.

What Is Body Image?

Body image is how you see your own body—and how you feel about how you look.

It includes:

- What you think when you look in the mirror
- How you feel about your weight, height, skin, hair, or shape
- Whether you feel proud, embarrassed, or neutral about your appearance

Body image is not just about looks—it's tied to how worthy, confident, and accepted you feel.

Why Does It Matter?

Because how you feel about your body affects your:

- Confidence
- Friendships
- Motivation
- Mental health

Negative body image can lead to:

- Anxiety or depression
- Eating disorders
- Low self-esteem
- Self-harm or social withdrawal

Positive body image helps you feel strong, capable, and at peace with who you are.

When Should I Care?

Right now.

If you:

- Compare yourself constantly
- Avoid mirrors, photos, or shopping
- Feel "ugly," "fat," "too dark," "too thin," or "not enough"
- Try dangerous diets, extreme exercise, or harmful habits

Then your body image may need healing—and it's okay to work on that.

Where Do These Feelings Come From?

Source	Impact
Social Media	Unrealistic beauty standards
Friends or classmates	Teasing, nicknames, comparisons
Ads, TV, influencers	"Perfect" bodies shown as ideal
Family comments	Pressure to be fair, slim, tall, etc.
Your own mind	Harsh self-talk and criticism

Who Decides Your Worth?
You do.
Not Instagram.
Not your relatives.
Not your followers.
Not a number on the weighing scale.

You are more than your looks. You are your kindness, ideas, skills, values, and spirit.

Real Voice

"Everyone at school used to call me 'moti' jokingly. I laughed it off at first, but slowly I started skipping meals. I hated my body. Then I found a fitness YouTuber who focused on strength, not size. I started lifting small weights, eating better—not to shrink, but to feel strong. That changed everything."
— Riya, 15, Indore

The Truth About Filters & Fake Perfection

• Most photos online are edited—brightened, reshaped, smoothed
• Angles, lighting, and posture change how a body looks
• People post highlights, not reality—no one shows their bloated days, breakouts, or sadness

Don't compare your behind-the-scenes to someone's showreel.

Signs of Negative Body Image

Mark the ones you've felt:

- I hate looking at myself in photos or mirrors
- I compare my body to others constantly
- I feel I'll only be happy if I "fix" something about my body
- I avoid swimming, dancing, or gym because of how I look
- I use filters to hide how I really look
- I've skipped meals, binged, or overexercised out of guilt

If you checked 3 or more, it's time to start healing—not your body, but your relationship with it.

Try This: Affirmation Mirror

Every morning, stand in front of a mirror and say:

- "My body does so much for me."
- "I deserve love, no matter my size or shape."
- "I am not just my appearance—I am smart, kind, and growing."
- "I choose to speak to myself with respect."

Say it even if you don't believe it yet. Your brain will learn the new language over time.

Body Positivity vs. Body Neutrality

Body Positivity	Body Neutrality
"I love my body no matter what."	"I accept my body and focus on what it can do."
Celebrates all body types	Removes obsession with appearance
Focuses on confidence	Focuses on function and freedom

You can choose either—or a mix. The goal is peace, not perfection.

Eating for Energy, Not Image

Diets, fasting, skipping meals, or bingeing are not the answer. Food is not your enemy.

- Eat to feel strong, focused, and nourished
- Choose balance: fruits, grains, proteins, water
- Don't label foods as "good" or "bad"—all have a role
- Don't punish yourself for enjoying food—it's part of life!

If food feels like a battle, talk to a trusted adult, counselor, or nutritionist.

Confidence Boosters Beyond Looks

Want to feel good without a filter? Try:

- Learning a new hobby
- Volunteering or helping someone
- Dressing in a way that feels like you
- Making a gratitude list
- Practicing posture—shoulders back, chin up
- Walking with music that makes you feel like a star

Confidence isn't about how you look. It's about how you carry who you are.

Follow Real, Not Just "Pretty"

Curate your social media:

Follow:

- Artists, activists, athletes
- People who inspire, not pressure
- Creators who show real, messy, beautiful life

Unfollow:
• Pages that make you feel "less than"
• Diet culture, toxic beauty standards
• Comparison-triggering influencers

Try This: Self-Esteem Journal

Answer these daily:
1. What's something I like about myself today?
2. What did my body help me do today?
3. Who am I beyond how I look?
4. One kind thing I said to myself today was: _______
5. One thing I want to thank my body for is: _______
Keep it private. Let it grow into your self-worth diary.

Busting Beauty Myths

× Myth	✓ Truth
"Fair is beautiful."	All skin tones are beautiful.
"Thin means healthy."	Health has nothing to do with size.
"Boys don't care how they look."	Boys also face body image pressure.
"Acne = dirty or unhealthy."	Acne is normal and common in teens.

"You must look a certain way to be loved." You're lovable just as you are.

NEP 2020 & Respecting Every Body

The National Education Policy supports:
• Inclusive and respectful environments in schools
• Life skills education that builds self-confidence and identity awareness
• Discouraging bullying and discrimination based on appearance

- Encouraging healthy lifestyle choices, not toxic ideals

You don't need to change your body—you need to change the lens you see it through.

Reflection Prompt

Write a letter to your body:

- Thank it for the things it does (breathing, dancing, thinking, healing)
- Apologize for times you were unkind
- Promise to treat it with more care and respect going forward

Your body is your lifelong home. Speak to it like a friend.

Key Takeaways

- Body image is how you see and feel about your body—not just how it looks
- Media, culture, and even loved ones can influence your self-worth
- Negative body image can affect your mental health and relationships
- You can build a kinder relationship with your body through small, daily practices
- You are not defined by your appearance—you are defined by your authentic self

Chapter 9

Loneliness & Peer Pressure

Introduction: Together But Still Alone?

You're surrounded by classmates in school. You have hundreds of contacts in your phone. You scroll through posts all day. And yet—you feel alone.

Loneliness and peer pressure are some of the hardest parts of being a teenager. Whether it's feeling left out, struggling to make real friends, or doing things you don't want to just to fit in—these experiences can affect your confidence and mental health deeply.

This chapter will help you recognize, understand, and cope with feelings of loneliness and the pressure to fit in, with strategies to build true connection and inner strength.

5Ws of Loneliness & Peer Pressure

Let's unpack these emotional experiences using the 5Ws framework.

What Is Loneliness?

Loneliness isn't just being alone—it's feeling emotionally disconnected even when people are around. It's the ache of feeling unseen, unheard, or misunderstood.

You might feel:
• Left out of groups or conversations
• Like no one "gets" you
• Disconnected from friends or family
• Isolated because of your interests, identity, or values

What Is Peer Pressure?
Peer pressure is the feeling that you need to act a certain way to be liked or accepted by others.

This could mean:
• Dressing like others
• Talking or behaving in a way that feels fake
• Saying "yes" to things you're uncomfortable with—alcohol, smoking, teasing, or risky behavior

It often comes from the fear of being excluded.

Why Do These Happen?
Because as humans—especially teens—you're wired to belong. Your brain is developing social skills and identity, so fitting in feels super important.
But when "fitting in" comes at the cost of authenticity or safety, it can hurt your mental health.

When Should I Be Concerned?

If you:
• Feel lonely or "different" most of the time
• Cry or feel empty after social events
• Constantly try to impress or please others
• Say "yes" even when you want to say "no"

• Feel guilt, regret, or shame after giving in to pressure

Then it's time to rebuild your support system and confidence.

Who Is Most Affected?
Anyone—**especially teens who are:**
• Introverted or shy
• New to a school or city
• Part of a minority group
• Not interested in "trendy" things
• Going through emotional or family struggles

Even people who seem popular can feel lonely or fake behind the scenes.

Real Voice

"Everyone in my class was part of a WhatsApp group except me. I found out when they posted about a hangout. I felt invisible. But later, I realized I didn't even enjoy the kind of jokes they made. I started spending time with two classmates who liked poetry like me. It wasn't many—but it was enough."
— **Aanya, 16, Bhopal**

The Mental Health Impact

Loneliness	Peer Pressure
Anxiety, sadness	Doing things against your values
Low confidence	Losing sense of self
Overthinking and rumination	Constant fear of rejection
Emotional withdrawal	Stress and guilt

Both can lead to depression, anger, or unhealthy behavior if not addressed.

Social Survival Tips

1. Learn to Set Boundaries

• It's okay to say:
"I'm not comfortable with this."
"No, thanks. I'll pass."
"That's not my thing."
Boundaries aren't rude—they're self-respect.

2. Know Your Values

Write down what matters most to you:
• Honesty?
• Creativity?
• Freedom?
• Family?
Let these guide your decisions—not others' expectations.

3. Don't Fear Being "Different"
Being unique is not a flaw. It's a superpower. The right people will appreciate the real you.

Try This: "How to Say No" Scripts

Situation	What You Can Say
Offered alcohol/smoking	"I'm good, I don't want that."
Pressured to make fun of someone	"Not cool—I'm not doing that."
Asked to copy in an exam	"I want to pass on my own efforts."
Forced to share private information	"I'm not comfortable sharing that."

Pushed to wear something revealing	"I like what I'm wearing, thanks."

Practice these in front of a mirror—it builds assertive confidence.

The Difference Between Alone & Lonely

Alone	Lonely
A choice	A feeling of disconnection
Can be peaceful	Feels painful or isolating
Helps recharge	Creates sadness or self-doubt
Happens to everyone	Needs emotional support and healing

Learning to enjoy your own company is a powerful life skill.

Building Real Connection

1. Focus on Quality, Not Quantity
One genuine friend > 100 "followers"

2. Join Clubs or Activities You Enjoy
When you engage in shared interests—sports, music, art—you meet people who get you.

3. Be the Friend You Wish You Had
- Listen without judging
- Celebrate others' uniqueness
- Reach out first—kindness is powerful

Social Media: Connection or Comparison?

Unhealthy Use	Healthy Use
Comparing lives & looks	Messaging someone you admire

Seeking validation from likes	Sharing something that excites you
Feeling worse after scrolling	Following inspiring creators
Online bullying or group exclusion	Muting or blocking toxic behavior

Take a break if scrolling makes you feel less than.

Try This: "Safe Circle" Worksheet

Draw a circle and place the names of:

- 2 people you trust deeply
- 1 adult you can turn to
- 1 person who makes you laugh
- 1 activity or place where you feel calm

This is your emotional safety net. Visit it when you feel lost.

Breathe & Ground When You Feel Left Out

Try the "5 Finger Grounding" method:

1. Touch your thumb to each finger, one at a time
2. With each touch, say: "I am here." "I am safe." "I am enough." "I belong." "I matter."
3. Repeat as needed.

This helps soothe the brain's rejection signals.

Busting Myths

× Myth	✓ Truth
"Everyone has a group except me."	Many teens feel disconnected inside.
"I have to fit in to be liked."	Being yourself attracts true friends.

“No one cares.”	People may not know you’re struggling.
“Saying no is mean.”	Saying no is self-respect.

NEP 2020 and Social-Emotional Learning

The National Education Policy encourages:

- Life skills education focused on self-awareness and peer interaction
- Inclusive classrooms where every child feels valued
- Peer mentoring and support groups
- Promotion of digital responsibility and empathy

You deserve to be included, respected, and authentic.

Reflection Prompt

Write about a moment when you felt pressured to do something you didn’t want to.

- What did you do?
- How did it feel?
- What would you do differently now?
- Who would support you if it happened again?

Key Takeaways

- Loneliness is emotional disconnection; peer pressure is social pressure to conform
- Both are common in teen life and can affect mental health
- Building self-worth, setting boundaries, and nurturing real connections help
- Saying no doesn’t make you rude—it makes you real
- You are not alone. The right people will love the real you

Chapter 10

Relationships & Mental Health

Introduction: Why Relationships Matter

We are social beings. Whether it's friends at school, family at home, or someone you like, relationships form a huge part of our life. They can lift us up—or weigh us down. As a teenager, relationships are complex. You're still figuring out who you are, and at the same time, you're trying to fit in, feel loved, and be understood.

But not every relationship is healthy. And when they get tough, they can deeply affect your mental health.

This chapter helps you understand how to build and maintain healthy relationships—and how to handle the ones that hurt.

5Ws of Relationships & Mental Health

What Are Healthy Relationships?

Healthy relationships:

• Make you feel safe, respected, and valued

• Allow open and honest communication
• Encourage you to be yourself

They are built on:
• Trust
• Boundaries
• Respect
• Empathy

Unhealthy relationships:
• Make you feel anxious, ignored, or controlled
• Involve constant criticism or manipulation
• Make you feel like you're walking on eggshells

Why Do Relationships Impact Mental Health?

Because emotions are involved. When you feel:
• Ignored by a friend
• Pressured in a romantic relationship
• Misunderstood by parents
...your self-esteem can take a hit. You may begin to doubt your worth, overthink every action, or feel emotionally exhausted.

On the other hand, supportive relationships:
• Act as a buffer against stress
• Boost your confidence
• Provide a safe space for expression

When Do Relationships Affect You the Most?
• During fights or arguments
• After a breakup or loss
• When someone disrespects your boundaries
• When there's peer pressure or comparison
• When trust is broken
Relationships matter most when you're feeling vulnerable. That's why

understanding emotional boundaries is crucial.

Where Can You Build Better Relationships?

Everywhere:

- At school (with classmates, teachers, peers)
- At home (with parents, siblings, relatives)
- Online (social media friendships)
- In your community (sports, hobby groups)

But remember: not every connection needs to be deep. Quality matters more than quantity.

Who Can Help When Relationships Go Wrong?

- A trusted adult
- A school counselor or psychologist
- A sibling or close friend
- Yourself—by stepping back and reflecting

It's okay to ask for help when things get confusing. You don't have to handle it all alone.

Types of Teenage Relationships

Let's explore the common ones:

Friendships

- Friends are your chosen family.
- Look for honesty, laughter, and support.
- Beware of fake friends who gossip, exclude, or manipulate.

Romantic Relationships

- Crushes and first loves are exciting—but can be confusing.
- A healthy relationship should never pressure you to do anything.
- Look for mutual respect, consent, and communication.

Family Relationships

• Parents may seem strict or out of touch, but they often act out of concern.

• Learn to express your needs calmly.

• Siblings may annoy you but can also be your biggest allies.

Online Friendships

• Real connections can happen online too—but be cautious.

• Never share personal information with someone you don't know in real life.

• Avoid relationships that cause comparison, jealousy, or low self-worth.

Red Flags in Relationships

• Constant criticism or insults

• Controlling behavior (checking your phone, choosing your friends)

• Guilt-tripping ("If you loved me, you would…")

• Gaslighting ("You're too sensitive" or "That never happened")

• Physical, emotional, or verbal abuse

If you see these signs, step back. You deserve better.

Try This: "Relationship Check-In"

Ask yourself:

1. Do I feel respected in this relationship?
2. Can I say "no" without fear?
3. Do I feel heard when I talk?
4. Am I being my true self?
5. Do I leave the interaction feeling lighter—or heavier?

If your answers are mostly negative, it might be time to set boundaries or seek help.

Boundaries: The Invisible Shield

Boundaries are rules you set to protect your peace. They could be:

• Emotional ("I don't like being made fun of, even as a joke.")

• Physical ("I need personal space.")
• Digital ("Please don't check my messages.")
Setting boundaries is not rude. It's self-respect.

Try Saying:
• "I need some space right now."
• "That joke hurt my feelings."
• "I'm not comfortable talking about that."

Building Healthy Relationships

Here are the ingredients:
1. **Trust** – Built over time through honesty
2. **Respect** – Treating each other as equals
3. **Communication** – Sharing, listening, understanding
4. **Support** – Being there in good and bad times
5. **Independence** – Giving space to grow individually

Mental Health & Breakups

Whether it's a romantic relationship or best friend fallout—breakups hurt.

You may feel:
• Rejected
• Alone
• Like something's wrong with you
But breakups are not the end. They're transitions.

How to Cope:
• Cry if you need to. Don't bottle it up.
• Talk to someone you trust.
• Avoid stalking their social media—it delays healing.
• Reconnect with hobbies and self-care.
• Know that the pain will fade. And you'll grow stronger.

Activity: Build Your "Safe Circle"

Draw a circle. In the center, write your name. Around it, list:
• 3 people you can trust
• 2 things you can do to calm yourself
• 1 place where you feel safe
This is your emotional emergency plan.

NEP 2020 Connection

The National Education Policy emphasizes:
• Life skills like emotional awareness, empathy, and communication
• Building safe and supportive school environments
• Inclusion of relationship and mental wellness education in the curriculum
Learning to manage your emotions and connections is now part of your education—and your wellbeing.

Reflect & Journal

• Who in your life makes you feel truly safe?
• Have you ever stayed in a toxic friendship? Why?
• What boundaries do you want to set going forward?
• How do you show respect in relationships?

Key Takeaways

• Relationships can be healing or harmful—know the difference
• Set boundaries to protect your peace
• Communicate openly and kindly
• Recognize red flags early
• It's okay to walk away from relationships that hurt
• Build a support system and reach out when needed

Chapter 11

Mindfulness & Everyday Calm

Introduction: Why Mindfulness Matters Now More Than Ever

Do you ever feel like your brain has 100 tabs open and all of them are buffering?

Between exams, messages, notifications, expectations, and your own thoughts, life can get overwhelming. That's where mindfulness steps in. It's not about "emptying your mind"—it's about learning to notice what's happening inside and around you without judging it.

This chapter will teach you the power of mindfulness—how to pause, breathe, and center yourself in a chaotic world. Think of it as a daily vitamin for your mental health.

5Ws of Mindfulness

Let's start by understanding mindfulness using the 5Ws framework.

What Is Mindfulness?

Mindfulness means being aware of what you're feeling, thinking, and sensing—right now—without trying to fix, fight, or judge it.

It's noticing:
• The way your breath feels when you inhale
• The sounds around you
• The emotions rising in your chest
• The thoughts dancing through your mind
It's being present, not stuck in the past or the future.

Why Is It Important for Teens?

Because your brain is going through rapid changes—and mindfulness:
• Helps you manage anxiety and mood swings
• Improves focus and memory
• Increases emotional regulation
• Boosts your ability to enjoy the small things
It's also a proven method used by athletes, CEOs, and even therapists to stay centered.

When Should I Practice It?

Anytime—but especially when:
• You feel overwhelmed or anxious
• You can't sleep
• You're stuck overthinking
• You want to calm down before an exam, performance, or conversation

Even 2 minutes of mindful breathing can reset your day.

Where Can I Practice Mindfulness?

Literally anywhere:
• While walking to school
• While brushing your teeth

• While eating
• Sitting in class
• Before sleeping

Mindfulness is about how you do things, not just what you do. You don't need a special place or mat.

Who Benefits From It?

Everyone. Teens benefit especially because:
• You're facing new emotions and responsibilities
• You're growing your identity and self-awareness
• You're bombarded with noise from the outside world
Mindfulness gives your mind a quiet, safe place to breathe.

Real Voice

"Before I discovered mindfulness, I reacted to everything. One rude comment would ruin my day. But after practicing mindful breathing for 5 minutes daily, I learned to pause before reacting. Now I choose my response instead of just reacting emotionally."
— Aditya, 17, Kolkata

3 Foundational Practices of Mindfulness

1. Breath Awareness
Sit quietly. Place a hand on your chest or stomach.
Breathe in slowly through your nose…
Feel the breath.
Breathe out through your mouth.

Notice:
• The coolness of air
• The rise and fall of your chest
• The pause between each breath

Try this for 1–2 minutes a day.

2. Body Scan
Lie down or sit comfortably.

Start from your toes and slowly move attention up:
- Notice your feet… ankles… legs… stomach… chest… arms… head
- If you feel tension, breathe into that spot
- Relax it gently, without forcing

This is great before sleep or after a stressful day.

3. Emotion Labeling

When a strong emotion hits, stop and name it:
- "I'm feeling anxious."
- "This is anger."
- "This is sadness."

Naming emotions reduces their intensity. It's like turning on the light in a dark room—you see things more clearly.

Guided Practice: Calm Playlist

Create a "Calm Playlist" with:
- Lo-fi beats or nature sounds
- Slow piano or acoustic music
- Affirmation tracks or guided meditations
- Indian classical ragas or flute music

Listen while walking, journaling, or winding down at night.

Try This: 5-Minute Daily Mindfulness Routine

Minute Activity
1 Sit still, close your eyes

2 Focus on breathing (in and out)
3 Notice sounds, smells, or sensations around you
4 Name one emotion you feel
5 Say an affirmation: “I am calm. I am here.”

Set a reminder. Practice daily for a calmer mind.

Common Mindfulness Misconceptions

× Myth	✓ Truth
“Mindfulness means clearing your mind.”	It means observing your thoughts without judgment.
“I need to sit cross-legged for hours.”	Even 1 minute counts. Do it your way.
“It’s boring.”	It becomes enjoyable as you get better at it.
“Only spiritual people do it.”	It’s a mental skill used by students, athletes, and professionals.

Everyday Mindfulness Activities

Activity	How to Make It Mindful
Eating	Notice the taste, texture, and smell
Walking	Focus on your footsteps and surroundings
Drawing	Observe colors, shapes, and motion
Brushing teeth	Notice each motion, the scent, the feel
Drinking water	Feel it move through your body

Mindfulness Apps for Teens

App	Feature
Headspace	Beginner-friendly meditations & animations
Smiling Mind	Designed for students & schools
Calm	Breathing tools, music, sleep stories
MyLife	Mood check-ins + recommended exercises
ThinkRight.me	Daily affirmations (India-based)

The Science of Stillness

Studies show mindfulness:

- Lowers cortisol (stress hormone)
- Improves sleep
- Reduces symptoms of anxiety and depression
- Boosts creativity and problem-solving
- Strengthens self-awareness and self-control

Practicing mindfulness is like going to the gym for your brain.

Reflection Prompt

Answer in your journal:

- What does "calm" feel like to me?
- When was the last time I felt truly present?
- What distracts me the most in a day?
- What's one small moment I want to be more mindful about tomorrow?

NEP 2020 and Mental Wellness in Schools

The NEP 2020 promotes:

- Social-emotional learning in classrooms
- Mindfulness practices during school hours
- Yoga, meditation, and life skills to support holistic development

• A focus on helping students be not just smart—but centered and aware
Mindfulness isn't extra—it's essential.

Key Takeaways

• Mindfulness is about being present in the moment without judgment
• It helps reduce stress, improve focus, and build emotional strength
• You can practice it anytime, anywhere—even for just a minute
• Small mindful habits (breathing, body scan, calm playlists) add up
• You don't need to be perfect—just begin

Chapter 12

Self-Care for the Digital Teen

Introduction: You Deserve to Feel Okay

Are you tired, stressed, or just emotionally drained—but can't figure out why?

You might be low on self-care.
In a world that's always online and always rushing, self-care often gets ignored. But it's not a luxury—it's a lifeline. Especially for teenagers like you, self-care helps build resilience, energy, and emotional stability. This chapter teaches you how to create a self-care routine that fits your life—without guilt, pressure, or a spa.

5Ws of Self-Care

Let's understand self-care using the 5Ws framework.
What Is Self-Care?
Self-care means doing things that support your physical, emotional, and mental well-being.

It’s not just bubble baths and yoga—it’s:

- Saying no to toxic people
- Getting enough sleep
- Eating nourishing food
- Spending time alone to reset
- Asking for help when needed

It's about being gentle and responsible with yourself.

Why Is It Important for Teens?

Because your mind and body are growing fast, and you're dealing with:

- Academic pressure
- Relationship ups and downs
- Hormonal shifts
- Social comparison
- Future anxiety

Self-care gives you the tools to cope with stress instead of breaking down.

When Should I Practice It?

Daily—not just when you’re exhausted.

Think of self-care like brushing your teeth. You don’t wait until they rot—you maintain them regularly.

- Morning = prepare your energy
- Afternoon = stay grounded
- Evening = recharge and unwind

Where Can I Practice It?

Anywhere. Your bedroom, school, garden, bathroom, bus ride—even inside your mind.

Self-care is about intention, not location.

Who Needs It?

Everyone. But especially:
• Teens juggling studies + social life
• People-pleasers who say yes to everything
• Overthinkers and perfectionists
• Anyone feeling low, burnt out, or invisible

You can't pour from an empty cup. Take care of you.

Real Voice

"I thought self-care was about taking breaks, but for me, it became about boundaries. I stopped saying yes to everything. I started sleeping properly, listening to music that calmed me, and keeping a simple checklist. That shift saved me during exam season."
— **Pranav, 16, Hyderabad**

The 6 Pillars of Teen Self-Care

1. Sleep Routine
• Aim for 8–9 hours of rest
• Avoid screens 1 hour before bed
• Try calming music or reading
• Use lavender oil, eye masks, or gentle lights

Try This: Set a phone alarm that says "Time to power down" at 9:30 PM.

2. Fuel Your Body
• Eat real food—grains, fruits, veggies, proteins
• Don't skip meals, especially breakfast
• Stay hydrated: aim for 6–8 glasses of water/day
• Avoid excessive junk, caffeine, and sugar

Try This: Create a weekly "Food Rainbow"—eat 5 colorful fruits/ veggies a day.

3. Move Daily

Movement = mental reset. It releases endorphins, lowers stress, and boosts confidence.

Options:

• Stretch in the morning
• Dance in your room
• Go for a short walk
• Do 10 jumping jacks before studying

Try This: "7-minute energy burst" routine once a day.

4. Mental Clean-Up

• Journal thoughts before bed
• Do a "brain dump" when stressed
• List 3 things you're grateful for each night
• Take 10 deep breaths in class when overwhelmed

Try This: Keep a mini "mood notebook" in your school bag.

5. Emotional Check-Ins

Ask yourself:

• How am I really feeling today?
• What do I need right now—rest, food, space, music, or support?

Try This: Use emojis to track your mood daily

6. Social Boundaries

Self-care means:

• Saying no to toxic group chats

• Taking phone breaks
• Avoiding gossip and negativity
• Recharging alone without guilt

Try This: Declare one evening a week as "Digital Detox Hour."

Your "Me-Time" Menu

Create a menu of activities that make you feel calm or energized:

Mood	Try This
Stressed	Breathe, stretch, color, listen to music
Lonely	Call a friend, hug a sibling, write a letter
Tired	Nap, drink water, take 5 slow breaths
Bored	Read something light, doodle, try a new app

Post this on your wall. Use it daily.

Monthly "Mood Check-In" Journal Template

Day	Mood (1–5)	Sleep	Energy	One Self-Care Act
Mon				
Tue				

At the end of the month, ask:
• What helped my mood the most?
• What made me feel off?
• What self-care practices worked best?

Apps to Support Self-Care

App	Best For
Fabulous	Habit building + morning routines
Daylio	Mood tracking + micro-journaling
Headspace	Sleep and mindfulness
Youper	Emotional awareness coaching
Calm	Music, stories, breathing

Reflection Prompt

Write honestly:
- What are 3 self-care habits I already do?
- What are 2 I want to try this week?
- What's stopping me from caring for myself more often?
- What belief do I need to let go of? (e.g., "I don't deserve rest.")

Affirmations for Self-Care

Say these aloud or write them down:
- "Rest is productive."
- "I am allowed to take care of myself."
- "My needs matter."
- "Saying no is a healthy choice."
- "I refill my cup so I can shine brighter."

NEP 2020 and Healthy Teen Habits

The NEP 2020 supports:
- Well-being over just marks
- Encouragement of restorative habits like yoga, sleep, nutrition, and exercise
- Life skills education that includes emotional health and time

management
• Creating space in schools for reflection and self-growth
You are not a machine—you are a human becoming.

Key Takeaways

• Self-care is daily maintenance for your mind and body, not a reward
• Teens need sleep, food, movement, and boundaries to stay mentally strong
• Little routines like breathing, journaling, and mood-tracking go a long way
• "Me-time" is not selfish—it's essential
• You deserve care, rest, and respect—especially from yourself

Chapter 13

When to Get Help – And How

Introduction: You Don't Have to Do This Alone

Sometimes, self-care isn't enough. Sometimes, talking to a friend doesn't help. And sometimes, no matter what you try, the sadness, fear, or confusion doesn't go away. That's when it's time to seek professional support—and there's nothing wrong with that.

This chapter is your guide to getting help—when to ask for it, how to do it, who to turn to, and what to expect. You're not broken. You're human, and asking for help is one of the bravest and healthiest decisions you can make.

5Ws of Getting Help

Let's break it down using the 5Ws framework.

What Does It Mean to "Get Help"?
Getting help means reaching out for support from a trained professional or a trusted adult when your mental health feels too heavy

to manage alone.

It includes:

- Speaking with a counselor, psychologist, or psychiatrist
- Calling a helpline or emotional support number
- Using mental health apps
- Joining a support group
- Talking to a teacher, parent, or trusted adult

It's not a sign of weakness. It's a step toward healing and hope.

Why Is It Important?

Because some emotional challenges—like anxiety, depression, trauma, or suicidal thoughts—require more than just willpower.

Professionals are trained to:

- Help you understand what's going on
- Teach you how to cope better
- Support you in feeling safe and stable
- Provide treatment if needed

Getting help earlier can stop problems from becoming worse.

When Should I Seek Help?

Ask for help if you:

- Feel sad, angry, or anxious most days for 2+ weeks
- Avoid people or activities you once liked
- Can't sleep, eat, or concentrate properly
- Have panic attacks, nightmares, or scary thoughts
- Use self-harm, substance use, or unhealthy habits to cope
- Feel hopeless, empty, or like you don't matter

You don't need to "hit rock bottom" to ask for help. The earlier, the better.

Where Can I Get Help in India?

Option	Description
School Counselor	Available in many schools; free and safe
Local Psychologist	Find via hospitals or clinics
Online Therapy	Affordable sessions via apps/websites
Government Helplines	Free and confidential (see list below)
Mental Health Apps	Tools for journaling, support, and reflection

Who Can Help Me?

Person	How They Help
Counselor	Offers emotional support and coping tools
Psychologist	Assesses and treats emotional/behavioral issues
Psychiatrist	Can prescribe medicine for mental health
Trusted Teacher/Parent	Provides guidance and connects you to help
Helpline Volunteers	Listen without judgment and offer next steps

Real Voice

"I used to think therapy was only for people with 'serious problems'. But after feeling numb for months, I talked to my school counselor. She listened without judging. It was the first time I felt seen. Now, I go once a week, and it's like cleaning out mental clutter."
— Sakshi, 17, Pune

What Is Therapy Really Like?

Therapy isn't about lying on a couch and crying while someone judges you.

It's a safe, private space to:
• Talk about your feelings
• Understand patterns in your thoughts and behavior
• Learn tools to cope better
• Feel supported and respected

First Session Checklist
• You don't need to know what to say
• You can be nervous—it's normal
• You're allowed to cry, pause, or take your time
• Everything you share is confidential (unless you're in danger)

Helplines and Support in India

Name	Contact	Type
iCall	9152987821 (Mon–Sat, 10 am–8 pm)	Emotional support (TISS)
AASRA	91-22-27546669 / 91-22-27546667	Suicide prevention helpline
Snehi	91-9582208181	Youth mental health support
Fortis Helpline	91-8376804102	For teens and parents
Mann Talks	1800-120-820050	Free, confidential listening

Save one or two in your phone right now.

What Not to Believe

× Myth	✓ Truth
"I'll be judged if I ask for help."	Professionals are trained to listen without judgment.
"Only 'crazy' people need therapy."	Everyone needs support sometimes.
"I should handle this on my own."	You're human, not a robot. You deserve help.
"It means I'm weak."	Asking for help takes strength and maturity.

Try This: "Asking for Help" Script

Not sure what to say? Try this:
"Hi, I've been feeling really overwhelmed and low. I'm not sure what to do, but I'd like to talk to someone who can help. Can you help me find a counselor or someone to talk to?"

Use this with:
• A parent or sibling
• A favorite teacher
• School principal or counselor
• A helpline volunteer
If saying it out loud feels hard, write it in a message or letter.

When a Friend Needs Help

If you're worried about someone:
• Gently ask how they're feeling
• Listen without interrupting
• Say: "You don't have to go through this alone."
• Offer to go with them to talk to someone
• Tell an adult if they mention harming themselves

Helping doesn't mean fixing them. Just be there and guide them to support.

What If My Family Doesn't Understand?

Many teens say:
• "My parents think I'm being dramatic."
• "They say just study harder or pray more."
• "They don't believe in therapy."

You can still:
• Talk to a teacher, school counselor, or helpline
• Use online therapy services (some are free)
• Build a support system of friends and trusted adults
• Educate your family slowly with videos, articles, or pamphlets

Your healing doesn't have to wait for everyone's permission.

Reflection Prompt

Write in your journal:
• What has been the hardest feeling for me lately?
• Have I tried handling it alone? Did it help?
• What would it feel like to let someone help me?
• Who is one person I can reach out to this week?

Key Takeaways

• Getting help is a brave and healthy response to emotional struggle
• Mental health professionals are trained to support without judging
• You can get help through school, helplines, apps, or private therapy
• You don't need to wait until things get worse—reach out early
• You are worthy of support, care, and healing

Chapter 14

Your Mental Health Toolkit

Introduction: Build Your Own Toolkit for Tough Days

Imagine going on a trek without a backpack. No food, no water, no map, no compass. That's what facing daily stress or emotional struggles without mental health tools feels like.

This chapter is about building your own toolkit—a collection of apps, habits, reminders, trackers, and practices that you can use anytime, anywhere. Like a first-aid box for your emotions and energy.

5Ws of a Mental Health Toolkit

Let's break it down using our trusted 5Ws framework.

What Is a Mental Health Toolkit?
It's a personal set of strategies, tools, and supports that help you manage your emotions, thoughts, and stress.

It can include:

• Breathing exercises
• Journaling prompts
• Mood tracking apps
• Helpline numbers
• Supportive friends or activities

Think of it as your emotional emergency kit.

Why Is It Important?

Because life can get overwhelming—exams, friendships, insecurities, rejection, panic attacks—and you need something to lean on in the moment.

A toolkit gives you:

• Confidence that you can handle difficult days
• Healthy options instead of unhealthy reactions
• A sense of control and comfort

It's a way to say: "I've got this."

When Should I Use It?

Anytime you feel:

• Anxious or overwhelmed
• Lonely or sad
• Confused or mentally stuck
• Drained or angry
• Out of balance emotionally

Also use it as a daily maintenance routine, not just when there's a crisis.

Where Should I Keep It?

Your toolkit can live in:

• A physical box or pouch at home

- A section of your phone or journal
- A list in your notes app
- A printed tracker on your wall

Wherever you can reach it easily when needed.

Who Should Have One?
Every teen. Whether you struggle with mental health or just want to grow stronger—this toolkit is for anyone who wants to thrive, not just survive.

Real Voice

"One night, I was spiraling with anxiety and couldn't sleep. I remembered my 'toolkit'—I pulled out my coloring book, listened to my Calm playlist, and wrote down 3 things I was grateful for. I still had anxiety, but I didn't feel helpless. That's the power of tools."
— Vanshika, 16, Delhi

What Goes Inside Your Toolkit?

Let's build it together—section by section.

1. Mood Tracker & Emotion Cards
Use a daily or weekly mood tracker:

Day	Mood (1–5)	Main Emotion	Trigger	Coping Tool Used
Mon		Anxious	School test	Box breathing
Tue		Calm	Music	Journaling

Create small emotion cards (angry, sad, joyful, anxious, excited). Pull one daily and reflect.

2. Calm-Down Strategies List

Situation	Try This
Racing thoughts	Box breathing, 5-4-3-2-1 grounding
Panic attack	Butterfly hug, safe space visualization
Anger	Walk it off, squeeze a pillow, journaling
Overthinking	Write it all out, tear the page, deep breath
Social anxiety	Practice your “safety script”, smile mantra

Tape this on your desk or school folder.

3. Playlists for Every Mood

- **Calm Playlist:** slow beats, instrumental, lo-fi
- **Confidence Playlist:** upbeat music that makes you feel powerful
- **Cry-It-Out Playlist:** for emotional release
- **Focus Playlist:** soft ambient music for studying

Use Spotify, YouTube, or build your own offline playlist.

4. Journaling Prompts

Write or voice record answers to:

- What do I feel right now—and why?
- What’s one small win I had today?
- What do I want to say but haven’t?
- What would I tell a friend feeling like this?

Keep a pocket diary or notes app titled “My Safe Space.”

5. Affirmations & Positive Notes

Print, write, or save:

- “I am doing my best.”
- “I am more than my mistakes.”

• “I am enough.”
• “This feeling will pass.”

Stick these near your mirror or in your notebook.

6. Apps & Tools Directory

App	Feature
Wysa	AI therapy chat + self-help tools
Fabulous	Habit building and energy tracking
Youper	Mood journal + AI coping guide
Headspace	Guided meditations, sleep sounds
Smiling Mind	Youth mindfulness program

Bookmark or install your top 3. Don’t overload.

7. People to Call in Crisis

Create a printed or digital list titled “My Lifeline Contacts”:

Name	Role	Number	When to Call
Mom	Parent	XXXX	When feeling overwhelmed
Neha Ma’am	School Counselor	XXXX	For anxiety or emotional talk
Snehi Helpline	Mental health support	9582208181	Anytime, free, private

Save them in your phone under a code name if needed.

8. Vision Board or Hope Jar

Vision Board:
• Images of your goals, quotes, dreams
• See it daily to stay focused

Hope Jar:
• Write down "reasons to keep going"
• Add to it on good days—read from it on tough ones

Printable Toolkit Page (Summary)

Create a one-page summary with:
• 3 tools that help me calm down
• 2 people I can call
• 1 app I like
• 1 affirmation I believe
• 1 action I'll take next time I feel stressed

Laminate or carry in your school bag.

Myths About Coping Tools

× Myth	✓ Truth
"If I need tools, I must be broken."	Everyone benefits from support tools.
"This stuff is too childish."	Even adults use grounding techniques.
"Only therapy fixes things."	Daily habits also heal and empower.
"I don't have time."	Most tools take just 2–5 minutes.

Reflection Prompt

Write in your journal:
• What tools already help me feel better?
• What new tool will I try this week?
• What does my emotional first-aid kit look like?
• What would my future self thank me for learning now?

NEP 2020 and Mental Wellness Resources

The NEP 2020 encourages:
• Life skills and emotional learning in the classroom
• Building student self-awareness and resourcefulness
• Creating access to mental health resources and referrals
• Normalizing tool-based emotional support as part of success

Having tools doesn't mean you're weak. It means you're prepared.

Key Takeaways

• A mental health toolkit is your personal support system
• It can include mood trackers, playlists, affirmations, coping lists, and contact sheets
• Use your toolkit during stress—or daily for wellness maintenance
• You are capable of creating safety and strength within yourself
• This is your backpack for life—keep it stocked and close

Chapter 15

Building Resilience for the Future

Introduction: What Doesn't Break You Can Teach You

Life is not always smooth. There are ups and downs, failures and wins, heartbreaks and healing. But what helps us move forward—even after hard times—is something called resilience.

This final chapter helps you understand what resilience really is, why it matters, and how to develop it like a superpower. Whether you're preparing for exams, facing rejection, dealing with mental health struggles, or just navigating life—you can build the strength to bounce back, grow, and thrive.

5Ws of Resilience

Let's understand resilience using our 5W approach.

What Is Resilience?
Resilience is your ability to bounce back from challenges, stress, or failures—without giving up or falling apart.

It doesn't mean:
• You never feel sad, anxious, or scared
• You always "stay strong" or "smile through pain"

It means:
• You learn to cope, adapt, and recover
• You grow through what you go through

Why Is It Important?
Because life will test you.

There will be:
• Difficult exams
• Friendship drama
• Failure or rejection
• Stress from expectations
• Mental health challenges

Resilience helps you:
• Face hard times with courage
• Stay calm under pressure
• Solve problems creatively
• Keep moving forward even after falling down

When Do You Need Resilience?

Every day, but especially when:
• You make a mistake or fail an exam
• Someone breaks your trust or heart
• You're bullied, misunderstood, or judged
• You feel mentally or emotionally exhausted
You don't need to wait for a "big crisis" to start building resilience.

Where Does Resilience Show Up?
• **In your thoughts:** "I will try again"

• **In your actions:** Getting back up after a tough day
• **In your habits:** Journaling, asking for help, breathing mindfully
• **In your relationships:** Not letting one fight destroy a friendship

It's not just about bouncing back—it's about bouncing forward.

Who Can Be Resilient?
Anyone.
Resilience is not a personality trait—it's a skill. And like any skill, it can be learned, practiced, and improved.
Even if you've felt fragile, sensitive, or easily stressed—resilience can grow in you with time, support, and intention.

Real Voice

"Last year, I failed my math board exam and felt like the world had ended. I cried for days. But then I started studying in a new way, reached out for coaching, and passed with 85% in the re-test. I didn't just bounce back—I learned more about myself than I ever had."
— Rishabh, 17, Jaipur

How to Build Resilience: 7 Proven Practices

1. Develop a Growth Mindset

Replace:
• × "I can't do this" → ✓ "I can't do this yet"
• × "I failed" → ✓ "I learned something"

Believing you can improve through effort and learning helps you recover faster.

Tip: Keep a list of "lessons I learned from setbacks."

2. Accept That Struggles Are Part of Life
Nobody has a perfect life—not even the influencers you admire.

Tough days don't mean:
- You're weak
- You're unlucky
- You've failed at life

It just means you're growing.

Tip: Write down 3 hard things you've faced—and how you survived.

3. Talk Kindly to Yourself
Your self-talk is your inner coach.

Instead of:
- × "I'm such a loser"

Say: ✓ "This is tough, but I'm trying my best."

Tip: Create your own "Compassion Mantra" to repeat when things go wrong.

4. Build Supportive Relationships

Resilience grows when you're not alone. Lean on:
- Friends who listen
- Family who encourage
- Teachers who guide
- Counselors who support

Tip: Create a "Resilience Circle" of 3 people you trust.

5. Practice Emotional Flexibility

It's okay to:
- Cry

• Feel stuck
• Be angry
Resilience doesn't mean "don't feel"—it means feel, deal, and heal.

Tip: Use emotion labeling ("I feel ___ because ___") in your journal.

6. Create Routines That Calm You
Chaos outside feels less scary when you have control inside.

Start with:
• A daily sleep-wake routine
• 15 minutes of movement
• 10-minute tech-free time
• Evening reflection or journaling

Tip: Make your own "Power Routine" for stressful days.

7. Visualize Your Comeback
Imagine yourself overcoming a fear, passing that exam, healing from heartbreak.
See it clearly in your mind. Feel the strength in your chest. Say it out loud.

Tip: Write a letter from your future self saying,
"Hey, you made it. You're stronger now. I'm proud of you."

Try This: The "Bounce-Back Plan" Worksheet

Fill in the blanks:
• **A time I struggled:** _______________
• **What I learned:** __________________
• **What helped me cope:** _____________
• **What I'll do differently next time:** _______________
• **One thing I'm proud of:** _______________
Hang it in your room as a reminder of your resilient self.

Myths About Resilience

× Myth	✓ Truth
"Strong people don't cry."	Crying is a healthy release.
"I should get over things quickly."	Healing takes time—it's not a race.
"Resilience means never falling."	It means getting up again and again.
"Some people are just born tougher."	It's a skill you can build like a muscle.

Resilience in Real Life

ScenarioResilient Response

You fail a test	**Review mistakes, seek help, re-prepare**
A friend excludes you	Process feelings, talk it out, set boundaries
You don't get into a dream college	Grieve, explore other paths, try again
You feel anxious about exams	Break study into chunks, use coping tools

Link to NEP 2020 Goals

The National Education Policy (NEP) promotes:

- Life skills and emotional strength
- Learning from failure as growth
- Self-awareness and stress management
- Building "whole individuals," not just test-takers

By practicing resilience, you're becoming a stronger student and citizen.

Reflection Prompt

Write in your journal:

- What has tested my resilience the most?
- How have I changed after a hard experience?
- What do I now believe about my own strength?

Key Takeaways

- Resilience means recovering and growing from tough times
- It can be built through mindset, habits, and support
- Everyone—including you—can become more emotionally strong
- There is no shame in struggling; strength lies in how you respond
- Your future will have challenges—but also courage, hope, and progress

Glossary

• Anxiety – A feeling of nervousness, worry, or fear that can affect your thoughts and body.
• Burnout – A state of emotional and physical exhaustion due to stress.
• Coping – Ways to deal with difficult thoughts and emotions.
• Depression – A mental health condition that causes deep sadness, low energy, and disinterest in life.
• Digital Wellness – Healthy use of technology to support mental well-being.
• FOMO (Fear of Missing Out) – The anxiety of being left out when you see others having fun online.
• Grounding – A calming method that brings your attention back to the present moment.
• Helpline – A number you can call for mental health support.
• Journaling – Writing down your thoughts and feelings as a way to understand yourself better.
• Mindfulness – Being fully present and aware of your thoughts, emotions, and surroundings.
• Mood Tracker – A tool to record how you feel each day.
• Panic Attack – A sudden wave of intense fear that causes physical

symptoms like fast heartbeats or shortness of breath.

• Resilience – The strength to recover from stress, setbacks, or difficulties.

• Self-Care – Actions you take to care for your mental, emotional, and physical health.

• Therapy – Talking to a trained mental health professional for support and guidance.

Book Summary

The Big Book of Mental Health for Teenagers is a friendly, practical, and easy-to-understand guide for young people navigating emotional challenges in a fast-paced digital world. Aligned with India's NEP 2020 and CBSE's Life Skills curriculum, it covers essential topics like anxiety, depression, panic attacks, body image, peer pressure, and digital wellness.

Each chapter follows a structured format using the 5Ws (What, Why, When, Where, Who) to simplify complex topics. The book is packed with self-help tools like breathing exercises, emotion trackers, checklists, "Try This" activities, and real-life stories. Whether you're struggling or simply want to grow emotionally strong, this book equips you with the knowledge, skills, and support you need to thrive.

Mental health isn't a luxury—it's a necessity. And this book is your toolkit for a brighter, braver, and healthier tomorrow.